His Poetry

WILL HARPER

You shall know the Truth,
and the Truth shall set you free.

—John 8:32

Table of Contents

About the Author

W ill grew up in Encino, California where his rebellion started at a young age. When Will was two years old, his father asked Will's mother why he ran away from him every time he came near. His mother responded, "Every time you see him you hit him." At five years, Will was fighting with his older brother and lost. As he ran crying to his mother, he put his arm through a glass pane in the door. This would be his first of many trips to the emergency room. Will fell in love with dirt bikes, and started racing at fifteen. He had natural talent and won the first of his three pro motocross championships by the time he was nineteen. The future looked promising for Will, but injuries forced him into retirement at the ripe old age of twenty-four. Will was not prepared for dealing with the loss of the only thing he ever really loved doing. Mad at the world, he went on a rampage, going to night clubs, drinking and snorting cocaine. Within a year, he was arrested for cocaine possession and got a one-year sentence in Los Angeles county jail. When he finished his time, Will decided to become a stuntman. He had two bad shoulders and two bad knees, but could still ride well enough to do stunts. Will became a top motorcycle stuntman, doubling Sylvester Stallone in "First Blood" and doing some major stunts on "The A Team" plus many other TV shows and movies. While working on a Mel Gibson movie "The River," disaster struck. Will was run over by a ten-ton truck, with twenty-five guys loaded in the bed. As the dual rear tires rolled over his chest, it sounded like dried tree branches snapping. Will, along with everybody else there, figured he was going to die. He didn't, although his injuries were severe – a broken neck, shoulder, ribs, elbow, plus torn muscles and internal injuries. During the recuperation process, Will decided to do something a little safer for a living, so he became a general building contractor. Construction was okay for making money, but Will missed the excitement of racing. Deciding four wheels would be safer, he started racing Karts. Will won many kart championships during the next two years, and then moved on to NASCAR Stockcars. After winning the track championship at Saugus Speedway two years in a row, it was time to move up to the NASCAR Southwest Tour. For three years Will struggled in the tour and never had the success expected. Will's older brother died during this time, and problems with his wife added to the darkness that was starting to come. At the end of the season in 1993, Will was burned out. He decided to take a year off and regroup. Although Will had not used drugs for over ten years, he drank alcohol and started drinking much more after quitting racing. Will knew why he quit using cocaine. Friends had lost everything, some had died, but at this dark point in his life, Will didn't care. He went to see an old friend that was losing everything due to his crack addiction and started smoking it himself. This was the beginning of a destruction run that would last over ten years and cost him everything he owned, and worse, everything he loved – his wife and five beautiful children. The ten-year run took him from LA to Maui, Charlotte, Las Vegas, back to Maui, to Kansas and finally the end of the road came (on a road) in Montana. Will had always run from his problems in the past, but this time he didn't. The reason? We'll let Will tell it in his own words.

The following is an excerpt from Will's life story.

"Snatched From The Fire"

Darkness surrounds this troubled life,
Heartless and cruel, malice and strife.

The destroyer of life, looks to devour
any that give… in to his power.

I was at the end of the road leading to death. Drugs
and alcohol had helped ease the pain of life, but the pain of
addiction was now worse than the original problems I was
hiding from. The police were looking for me, with a warrant
for distribution of meth, which carries a maximum penalty
of one hundred years in prison and a one hundred thousand
dollar fine. Things were getting darker by the minute. The
fact that my wife was already in custody, and my six month
old son was in protective custody didn't help either. I didn't
know what to do, or where to go. It was at this darkest
moment of my life that a strange thing happened. In my
mind I saw myself getting arrested at the very place I was
driving to. It was so vivid it seemed real. I knew I couldn't go
there, so I decided I would hide in the woods. This is where
things get very strange.

As I'm getting ready to head into the woods, something
tells me not to, but to go on and be arrested, and it will be
okay. At this point I say "I'll go, and if I get arrested as I'm
seeing in my mind, that will be God's answer for me." This
was a strange thing for me to say, since I really didn't know
God at that time. I believed in God, but I had never read the
Bible, and had only gone to church a few times (unwillingly I
might add). I started driving to the gas station and something
started happening that I didn't understand at the time, but I
felt a peace come into my heart that I had never known. This
didn't make any sense since I was very paranoid from the
years of crack cocaine and meth use. As I got out of the truck,
I saw a sheriff cruising down the highway and he looked me
right in the eye just as if someone was telling him, "There he
is!" Within minutes, the vision I had seen earlier unfolded

right before my very eyes. I had been arrested a few times in my life, but never by so many cops, and definitely not with the feeling of peace that I felt that day. Being arrested is usually a situation filled with anger, anxiety, and despair, but not this time... I knew something inside me had truly changed. I knew I had been arrested by God.

Will came to faith in Jesus Christ during his incarceration at the Ravalli County jail in Hamilton, Montana. His book of poetry tells of the change God brought about in a man that struggled with life and the trials that life brings. It tells of the power that saved Will from death and gave him life. Will now spends his time sharing the good news of Jesus Christ, sharing his testimony, and helping others facing life's trials by looking to Jesus instead of the world. He is involved with the ISAAC'S HOUSE, a faith-based program that helps prepare men to live life centered in Christ.

Cycle News, May 1975: Will Harper makes come-back after shoulder surgery

Cycle News, June 1975: Will Harper was the one in the 250 Pro class, as nobody could get near enough to him to breathe his exhaust fumes

Cycle News, March 1981: Will Harper wins both motos in the 500 Pro class at Saddleback Park

Will Harper wins Professional Kart Championship at Saugus Speedway in 1985

Will & pit crew celebrate winning track championship
at Saugus Speedway

Will racing on the NASCAR Southwest Tour
at Phoenix International Raceway

This photo & those on the back cover:
Will doing stunts for the TV Show *The A Team*

His Poetry

*W*hat is the Truth? Jesus Christ! I could never see this before because I was in the dark. Reading was the light I needed to be able to see the Truth. I was sitting in jail in Montana facing one hundred years in prison on drug charges, so I decided to start reading the Bible for the first time in my life. I believed in God but didn't know much about Him. It didn't take long for God to make Himself known to me. He changed my life so completely that I knew my old life was gone and that I had been truly born again. At the moment I came to believe that Jesus was the Son of God and that He died for me, I broke down and started crying. It seemed like a lifetime of tears were flowing out of me. When they stopped I picked up my pencil and–not really thinking about what I was do-ing–started to write a poem. I wasn't a poet. I really didn't care for poetry. But the next thing I knew, there was a poem on the paper. Many more poems followed in the next few years. I decided to put them in a book with some of the thoughts that inspired them. As I went through the process of incarceration, I also went through the process of sanctification. The prison process is now over, but the sanctification process is ongoing. As Paul said, "Not that I have laid hold of it yet; but one thing I do: forgetting what lies behind and reaching forward to what lies ahead, I press on toward the goal for the prize of the upward call of God in Christ Jesus." (Philippians 3:12-14 NASB). These poems usually came to me after a Bible study. I would be meditating about the lesson when a peculiar feel-ing would come over me. I knew it was probably a poem coming. It is interesting that I can't write these poems until God sends them. I have tried; it doesn't work. At first I had trouble understanding what was going on, but after a year or so, He sent this poem to help me accept the gift of His poetry with peace and grace.

Poems From Heaven

A poem from heaven came today
I love to hear what God will say
Don't think too hard; His spirit will
Write this poem when my mind's still
With His help, the words flow free
They come from Him, not from me
So if I boast, it's in the cross
Worldly gain, I count as loss
I love the grace of His rhyme
I am amazed every time
A poem is sent from God above
Filled with joy, peace and love

7-7-2005
Great Falls Regional Prison

"Saved" was the first poem that came. I was excited about the change I felt, filled with the Holy Spirit, and thinking for the first time that I had hope for the future. My wife was in the same jail, facing the same long sentence. I knew that God loved us and somehow everything would be O.K.

Saved

I was saved today; the tears flowed free
Accepting the love God has for me
I thought of you, my beautiful wife
So happy now, we'll have a life
We are apart, for how long unknown
With God's love, our seed is sown
With all my love, I pray for you
Knowing inside, He loves you too
With His love, we'll make it through
The stormy life we both knew
He forgives our sin; we can't help but win
The struggle to be a family again

7-23-2004
Ravalli County Detention Center

I studied the Bible constantly for the next six months. For three of these months, I was allowed out of jail to go to a place called Isaac's House where I learned about living life using biblical principles. I was hoping I would be allowed to continue, but instead I was sentenced to ten years in Montana State Prison at Deer Lodge. As I sat back in jail waiting to be transported to prison, I was surprised at the peace I had. Here I was going to prison, and what normally would have been the worst day of my life was actually a day filled with hope for the future and excitement at what God would be doing in my life while I was doing my time.

Ten Years

O Lord, help me do this time
With Your Spirit helping mine
All the things I thought I'd need
All are vanities, the flesh to feed
Help me now to do Your will
Souls to win, flesh to kill
How I love to do Your plan
Walk with You, a brand new man
Soon I leave this county jail
On to Deer Lodge, send my mail
I trust in You; I'm in Your care
At home or chained, Your cross I bear

1-14-2005
Ravalli County Detention Center

I was excited about what God had done in my life, and I wanted to share the good news with others. It was sad to see the lack of interest, but I understood it because I had been there myself. I wondered how I could get some of these guys to take a look. A few did, but I soon realized I would not be leading everyone in the jail to Christ.

The Blood of Christ

Why do you fear? God is so near
You want to believe
Instead you will grieve
With no faith in Him, life is so grim
I was such a man; from the Bible I ran
I never could see, God's love would be
In one honest book, if only I'd look
Pride starts to grumble
God wants us humble
He takes away grief, by our belief
For what is not seen, look in between
The pages of truth–pure love, as in Ruth
It's plain as can be; Christ died for me
With blood He has paid
for transgressions made
By God's graceful way, His Son did pay
all of our sin, paid for by Him
A gift from above, an act of pure love
Still want to grieve, or will you believe?
In death you won't pay; the Son is the way

1-16-05
Ravalli County Detention Center

$\mathcal{O}$nce I got to prison, I spent two months in a place called Reception, locked down twenty-three hours a day. We had one hour out to shower and walk around in an area a little bigger than a tennis court. I had plenty of time to think about and pray for what God was doing. I had big plans for my prison ministry, but I was looking past what God was teaching me right then. The two months I was in Reception helped me learn to pray more and trust in God's plan.

Reception

Thank you, Lord, for this time
In Your plan, not in mine
With love and hope, I do Your will
By Your grace, my heart is still
Anxious thoughts have gone away
In Your care, I will stay
With Your Spirit, help me speak
In Your will to help the weak
I praise You as You strengthen me
Through Your love, I am free
Some here feel they're locked away
From Your love, they did stray
I pray through me, they will hear
Your call to them becoming clear
Then Your voice is heard on high
We look to You above the sky
We're filled with love, no longer mad
Removing things that made us sad
Born again, a brand new seed
I praise You Lord; we're free indeed

2-24-05
Montana State Prison

I had been thinking about how Jesus paid the price of sin not just for me but for all mankind. I thought of all the different people at the cross, and of Peter denying that he even knew Him. I wondered where I would have been had I been there. It was at this point I realized that every type of person was there, so I figured we were all there. We might not actually have been at the cross but Christ was, and in our place.

We at The Cross

We were all there
In sinful despair
With blood He did pay
For our sin that day
Not understanding ... that God was demanding
The payment for sin ... to all fall on Him
Three times was denied; The shadows can't hide
Even this He forgave, with love that does save
Totally forsaken
His life was taken
Rose on the third day
"It is I," He did say
So we could all know
He came back to show
That He will come back
Don't let your faith lack
It could be this year
I know He is near
We're crucified in Him
And now born again
Look to Him high above
We're saved by His love

3-29-2005
Montana State Prison

*E*arlier in life I had seen Christians that had problems, and I was quick to point out what hypocrites they were. Now that I was a Christian I couldn't help notice that the actions of some Christians were not lining up with my understanding of God's Word. As I wrote this poem, God faithfully pointed out that my heart toward these people was not in accordance with His Word. He also warned me with this Bible verse:

> "So if you think you are standing firm,
> be careful that you do not fall."
> 1 Corinthians 10:12 NIV

Total Surrender

It's what God requires
Not worldly liars
Who think they're not seen
They sin in between
The sermon on Sunday
Adultery on Monday
This evil, God sees
Cheap talk won't appease
So don't even start
God knows your heart
Be born again
Surrender to Him

5-20-2005
Great Falls Regional Prison

I knew what being in Christ meant, but I found myself not always walking in the Spirit. I thought about the verses that meant so much to me in this aspect of being a Christian. Romans 6:5-7 tells us that we are united with Christ in the likeness of His death and resurrection, and that we should consider ourselves dead, or free, from sin. Galatians 2:20 says, "I have been crucified with Christ; and it is no longer I who live, but Christ lives in me; and the life which I now live in the flesh I live by faith in the Son of God, who loved me and gave Himself up for me." My pastor, Jim Landis from Isaac's House, had spent weeks going over these verses with me until I had a full knowledge of the importance of being in Christ. As I thought about all these things, the following poem came. It is one of my favorites, and I read it quite a bit in prison when I needed a reminder that I am in Christ.

In Christ

United with Him, in death and in life
The blood of the cross, took away strife
Looking to Christ, crucified to sin
Alive in His love, I am born again
Although I'm in prison, He helps me be
Peaceful and happy–it's like I am free
I live in the Spirit, do things I should
Christ is the difference; God is so good
My old life is gone, no longer a slave
The evil one beckons–I don't even wave
The perfecter of faith, keeps my heart still
Longing to please Him, delight in His will
I am in Christ, hidden in God
Happy in prison; some find it odd
What they don't know, comes from above
I am set free, by His perfect love

5-25-2005
Great Falls Regional Prison

$\mathcal{S}$tudying the Word of God during my time in prison helped me in so many ways. I thought about my old life, and even though I was in prison, I was happy to be alive. Not just alive according to the world, but *truly* alive, with a peace and love that I never knew.

Alive to Praise

Heavenly Father, I praise You
Peace and love, I never knew
For I searched through Your Word
You called to me and I heard
Your love had picked up my soul
Freed from death's deep, dark hole
Your light is shining in my life
Grace abounds; gone is strife
Delighting now in Your will
Obeying You is my thrill
It's Your will I long to do
Thank You, Lord–all praise to You

5-24-05
Great Falls Regional Prison

$\mathcal{O}$ne day some bad news came about a guy who had been in Ravalli County Detention Center with me. He had struggled about being locked up, but he was studying the Bible. I thought things would get better for him. So much stuff that was hard to take (especially in jail) got dumped on him that he took his own life. It was sad to think how close he was to knowing the One who could have given the strength he needed to get through those trials.

The Joy of Trials

Consider it all joy, my friend
The trials perfect us, in the end
Don't look too hard for relief
Accept the test, faith and belief
Endurance gained through the test
Makes us perfect–God knows best
Faith in God, our strength in trials
Peace in Christ reaps big smiles
Suffering here makes us strong
The Lord decides for how long
By His plan, our paths are laid
This is the day the Lord has made
Don't complain; enjoy the test
Soon you'll enter into His rest

6-5-2005
Great Falls Regional Prison

$\mathcal{I}$t had been a year since I felt God called me to stop running and surrender to Him. I looked back and saw such a big difference in my life. I remembered the conversation I had with God and thought about the wretched condition I was in then and how faith in Him had given me a new life. I had trusted in worthless things to live my life, but now I felt the urge to acknowledge God for what He had done in my life and, as Joshua had done, make a statement that I would serve Him.

The Conversation

One year ago, You said to me
"Come unto Me. I'll set you free."
Arrested and jailed was a bad scene
Safely with You, I was serene
You built me up, strong in your grace
Putting a smile back on my face
As time goes by, reading Your Word
Peace in my heart, Your Spirit stirred
You built me up, free in Your grace
Strength comes from You for trials I face
Some trust in chariots, others a horse
The battle is won by You, of course
The rest of my life, it's You I turn toward
As for me and my house, we'll serve You, Lord

6-20-2005
Great Falls Regional Prison

*B*ad choices had caused much grief in my old life. In this new life, I found that choices still needed to be made, but they were of a different kind. The choices I now faced were more of a spiritual nature. Before I was saved, I made choices thinking only about existing in this world from day to day. Now I was thinking about eternity.

The Choice

He can't love us less and can't love us more
Our choice leads to heaven or down to earth's core
Why do we fight, resisting His love
He patiently guides from heaven above
The choice seems so simple, when reading God's Book
Why do we listen when Satan says, "Look!"
The more that we look to God's graceful ways
The more that we reap the goodness He pays
As we are strengthened in Christ, we are bold
Knowing we'll walk on streets paved with gold
The peace we now feel, accepting God's grace
Gives us the strength for trials we face
We make the right choice; in Christ we are free
Our light will break out; good days we will see

7-14-05
Great Falls Regional Prison

$\mathcal{M}$aking a choice seems so simple, but making the *right* one didn't always happen. I had just read *70 x 7 and Beyond,* the Monty Christensen story, which tells of the patience of God's grace. It made me think of how patient God is with us as we do things our way and fall. He lovingly picks us up time after time.

Grace

The beauty of the Lord's grace
Free to all the human race
Perfect love, forgiving all
He catches us when we fall
As we stumble, once again
He loves us, but hates the sin
Deserving death, we misbehaved
By His grace, we are saved
Once again, we go our way
"Help us, Lord," we turn and say
Again, by grace, He will forgive
The godless way we choose to live
Amazing grace, the blind will see
Heals the sick and sets us free
His loving grace–the gift revealed
By His grace, we are healed
All life's trials we can face
Strengthened by His loving grace

7-19-2005
Great Falls Regional Prison

*W*hile thinking about the grace of God and how many times He forgives us, a young man came to my cell and said that he wanted to accept Jesus Christ. I had never led any one to Christ, so I found a Bible tract with the sinner's prayer and led him to Jesus. Afterwards I was thinking about what had happened there in my cell and felt the need to pray the sinner's prayer myself. It came out like this.

Sinner's Poem

Heavenly Father, I come to You
Confessing that sin is all that I do
I ask for forgiveness by Your pure grace
Cleansing my sin, not leaving a trace
Your Son, I accept, as Lord in my life
I know that He died for me and my strife
No greater love can anyone show
He died for my sins–this I now know
You raised Him up on the third day
He is the Truth, the Light and the Way
Repent from the old; new life can start
I praise You for a repentent heart
No longer a slave, free from all sins
By Your free gift, new life begins
A life of good works sounds good to me
Then on to heaven for eternity

7-22-2005
Great Falls Regional Prison

*M*y time at Great Falls Regional Prison was a time of learning and growing in God's grace. I now think back on the freedom from outside influences and the busyness of life during my stay there and realize what a blessing it was. Where else, or when, would I ever be able to study God's Word without interruption as I did then? As I think about how peaceful my days were, in a place that was anything but peaceful, I know I was blessed with peace and truly in His care.

Praying in Jesus

It is the high point of my day
When grace and love come my way
I love to hear Your spirit speak
It is Your will I long to seek
I praise You for all You do
Thank You, Lord; I love You
As I pray for a friend
I feel the blessing that You send
When I tell You of my sin
You forgive me, once again
As I pray in Your will
Grace abounds; my heart is still
I start my day in Your plan
Your grace guides a new man
Through the day, I know You're here
I stop and pray, drawing near
At night I pray before I sleep
I know I'm safe, my soul You keep
Awakened to a brand new day
I look to You to point the way
Thank You, Lord, for Your prayer
Blessed with peace, in Your care

1-2-2006
Great Falls Regional Prison

$\mathcal{M}$y cell was the Bible study and prayer cell. At 8:00 every night we would meet for prayer. One day we got a letter from the grandmother of one of the guys. She was giving us words of encouragement for our prayer time and study of God's Word. She told us that she and fifty-seven other prayer warriors were praying every night at 8:00 for us! This felt really good to hear and lifted our spirits. Sometimes a feeling comes over you in prison that your friends and family and society in general don't want anything to do with you. It can really bring someone down. These ladies did what they could by praying for us and visiting with us through their letters. Jesus said it is like visiting Him when we visit even the least important person in prison (Matthew 25:39-40). I didn't know at the time, but when I got out of prison I found out that so many people I didn't even know were praying for me. It made me wonder how many other things God has done for me that I don't know about.

Praying Saints

Thank You, Lord, for saints who pray
In Your grace and in Your way
Their prayers are filled with such love
Sent from You, up above
They pray for us, locked away
Yes, they're faithful, every day
For they answer when You call
Praying prayers for us all
I feel their love, Spirit-filled
For they do what You have willed
They pray for us as we grieve
Helping us come to believe
Bless them, Lord, in every way
These loving saints, as they pray

2-26-2006
Great Falls Regional Prison

*T*he great news came that I would be going to pre-release as an inmate worker. I know prayer had a lot to do with that. Before pre-release I had to go back to Montana State Prison for drug treatment. That meant going through Reception again, but that didn't matter because I could feel God's love in my heart and the peace that only He can bring.

I Feel God's Love

I feel God's love pour down like rain
Cleansing my soul, easing my pain
He is the Light; He is the Way
He is the Truth; I will not stray
So when I search, I look above
Feeling the touch of His perfect love
Peace comes through Him, sent down to me
Here in my cell, He sets me free
Oh, how I love God's perfect grace
Flowing through me here in this place
The peace that He brings will get us through
The trials we face, both me and you

5-7-2006
Montana State Prison

God replaced the hate in my heart with love. I was grateful for this gift because hate used to bring me down and wear me out. I remember struggling with the hate I held onto when I first got to jail and how everything seemed to get better after the heart-change God gave me.

The Gift of Love

Of all God's gifts, the best is love
Sent to us from Him above
Other gifts will fade away
Only love is here to stay
Love is patient; love is kind
Love will heal the heart and mind
God is love; that's understood
To feel His love is so good
Love is strong, and will revive
A soul once dead, comes alive
You sent Your Spirit filled with love
Upon the wing of a dove
I feel Your love in my heart
Accepting You was the start
Loving all, in this way
Love feels good every day
Love is peace; gone is strife
For love is the gift of life

5-22-2006
Montana State Prison

The change from prison to pre-release was nice. It was another step in the process of being closer to freedom. I saw some of the guys mess up and go right back to prison. Others progressed a while before they lost it. Some went all the way through the pre-release program with very few problems. I wanted to make it, so I asked God to show me the way.

Show Me The Way

I look to You every day
So I don't lose my way
On my own, I did no good
Without You Lord, alone I stood
You said to me, that fateful day
"Follow Me. I am the Way."
Surrendering, then and there
My life was now in Your care
I am changed by Your grace
Your kingdom is a peaceful place
I feel Your love every day
For You show me the way

7-1-2006
Pre-release Center
Montana Correctional Services

*P*re-release is designed to test people and see how they react to hard situations. I know the "old me" would have had a hard time with the "unfairness" of the rules, and then used this perceived wrong as an excuse to do wrong. I can now look back and see that God had strengthened me with His grace. No longer looking for reasons to do wrong, but actually accepting anything that came my way with a smile and peace in my heart that only comes from the grace of the Lord.

The Grace of The Lord

Oh how I love, the grace of the Lord
Lifting me up, my spirit has soared

Loving and healing, in His kind touch
He is my Savior, I love Him so much

He gives me peace, my heart is still
A blessing to me, by His kind will

This gift of grace, He gave to me
Cost Him so much, to us it is free

A gift not deserved, He freely gives
So he who was dead, now truly lives

10-29-06
Pre-release Center
Montana Correctional Services

I was going to a Christ-based addiction recovery group where I heard many people struggling with forgiveness. It got my attention because it seemed like the ones that had a hard time forgiving were the same ones that struggled in recovery. One of the guys that had been sober for years tells how he would just say over and over, "I choose to forgive." He would keep saying it until it happened, and he told us it always worked. Sometimes it would take longer, but it always worked for him. As I thought about it, I thought of Jesus choosing to forgive, and I'm so grateful He did!

I Choose to Forgive

An innocent Man died in my place
Forgiveness and love, beautiful grace
He died for *my* sin, setting me free
Forgiving my debt for eternity
Let me forgive the hurt and the loss
You showed me how, nailed to the cross
Asking the Father from Your pure heart
Forgiveness for me and a new start
You paid the price; now I can live
You help me say, "I choose to forgive."

5-18-2007
Pre-release Center
Montana Correctional Services

Thanks, KJ!

I knew on my own that I couldn't forgive my enemies or do any of the things Jesus tells us to do. I thought of the power He gives me to live right. I had been so weak just three years ago, unable to stay sober for any length of time. It made me think of who Jesus is to me.

Who Jesus Is to Me

The Word of God, truth and grace
Savior of the human race
Peace and love He brings to me
From my chains, He set me free
King of kings, faithful, true
Lord of lords, through and through
With the Father, up above
Sends His Spirit–filled with love
His grace and love give perfect peace
The light of God will never cease
Jesus fills me every day
He is the Truth, the Light and Way

6-25-2007
Isaac's House

$\mathcal{O}$n completion of pre-release, I was free to start back to work as a general building contractor, but I felt God was guiding me in a different direction. I prayed about where He was leading me and was certain it was back to Isaac's House. I felt that He would use me to help other guys that were going through the same problems I had gone through. Psalm 23 came to mind as I thought about how God had protected me and led me out of the valley of death.

My Shepherd

He is my Shepherd, safe in His love
Gently He leads, guides from above
Having no want in pastures so green
By the still waters, a heavenly scene
My soul is restored; His path is the way
In His righteous name, always I pray
The valley of death, I will not fear
Though evil lurks, I know You are near
Your staff and rod, they comfort me
My table's prepared, before my enemy
Anointing my head, my cup overflows
Goodness and mercy forever follows
All of my days, I'll dwell with You
My Lord and my Savior, faithful and true

8-13-2007
Isaac's House

$\mathcal{I}$t had been two and a half years since I had been at Isaac's House, and it felt good to be back. On Sunday I shared with the church how good it was to be back and thanked them for all their prayers and letters. I realized that although I had been away for over two years, we had been connected during this time by Christian love.

Christian Love

Connected by birth
In this new life
Sticking together
Through all of our strife
Sisters and brothers
More than a friend
Our love for each other
Having no end
One common thing
Makes us all friends
The love in our hearts
That Jesus sends
When we're apart
With miles in between
Our hearts are connected
By what is not seen
Invisible strands
God pulls from above
Gives us this gift
Of Christian love

12-7-2007
Isaac's House

"Depart from Me I never knew you" is something I pray I will never hear. I pray nobody else hears it either. When Jesus said these somber words, He was talking to people that thought they were doing great works in His name. Jesus also said, "He who has My commands and keeps them is he who loves Me." He also commanded us to love one another. I can't help but think of the people that are so hard to love and how we struggle with the command to love one another. If we aren't truly loving one another, even the unlovely, we are transgressing the commands of God and in real danger of hearing "Depart from Me."

"Depart from Me"

I am saved, you may say
Why then do you not obey?
It is hard to understand
Your lack of love for this command
"As I loved you, love one another"
Then you turn and slay your brother
If God's commands are a bother
I have to wonder who's your father
I fear you'll hear "depart from Me
You doer of iniquity!"

11-2-2008
Hamilton, MT

While praying one morning, I was led to ask God to cleanse me of anything that would cause me to stumble. He brought to mind that I am a clay jar and He would cleanse me. As that thought went through my prayer, I could picture a shiny jar that was very clean. I cried out, "Oh Lord, let me be like that jar, cleansed and ready to be filled with Your Spirit." I could feel His Holy Spirit filling me, and I knew He was leading me to write a poem. The words "clay jars" came to mind and I felt the urge to stop praying and go to the computer to see if God was giving me a poem. I wasn't sure if I should stop praying and go try, so I asked, and I heard, "Go!" I ran to the computer and started writing "Jars of Clay." I was amazed how God was writing the poem even though my eyes were closed part of the time. When I felt the poem was finished, I read it and thought it was a wonderful poem, so I emailed it to a few people, and then I thought I felt another poem coming on. My friend Kezia had talked about a verse that was coming to mind but I couldn't remember what it was, so I called her and she gave me some verses. As I looked at one of the verses, I realized God had orchestrated a scenario to get the poem "Jars of Clay" finished the way He intended. Not only did He intend for another verse to complete the poem, but He also wanted to involve another saint to accomplish His work. It was a good example of how He can use us, the body of Christ, to accomplish His purpose.

Jars of Clay

A temple of God is what we are
No place for cattle and thieves
We fill ourselves with worldly things
And wonder why He grieves

Search our hearts, we ask the Lord
He comes with zeal and might
Turning the tables, of deceit
He starts to make us right

The cleansing sometimes painful
As Jesus does His work
With zeal He cleans His Fathers house
Where evil cannot lurk

Some of us were blind or sick
Others weak and lame
To heal and cleanse us of our sin
For this work He came

After He cleansed the temple
Calmly He sat to teach
Filling empty jars of clay
Made ready for outreach

No longer filled with things of man
We are Holy jars of clay
Temples cleansed for noble use
To glorify His Way

His Light now shining in our hearts
Treasure in fragile jars
We serve Him as saints of Light
For us He bears the scars

9-25-2008
Hamilton, MT

$\mathcal{W}$hile reading Psalm 26, I thought of how much God had done for me. Verse 7 tells of thanksgiving, and verse 12 of now standing on solid ground and publicly praising God for it. This really spoke to my heart as I thought of where I had been and where God had brought me. It is my prayer that God will speak through these poems to the heart of anyone that is suffering or struggling in this life. And may the love of God through Jesus Christ strengthen and empower you to stand on solid ground.

Sanctuary

I come to Your altar, O Lord
Singing a song of thanksgiving
I praise You, my everlasting God
You brought me to the land of the living
For I was in bondage, deep in my sin
A prisoner in chains, waiting to die
As I moaned in the darkness
It was You who heard my cry
So I will praise You, O Lord
And tell of Your kindness and grace
For I now stand on solid ground
Here in Your sanctuary, with You
Face to face

2-2-2008
Isaac's House

The purpose of Isaac's House (Instructing Saints All About Christ) is found in Colossians 1:28: "And we proclaim (to make known, to teach, to speak of) Him (that is Christ), admonishing (to warn, to motivate to a proper course of action) every man and teaching (to explain, to impart instruction) every man with all wisdom (the knowledge and practice of the requisites for godly and upright living), that we may present every man complete (mature, achieving the full measure of human integrity and virtue, lacking nothing necessary for completeness) in Christ."

Providing an opportunity for men to be trained in Spiritual Disciplines so they can be a productive member and a positive influence upon society as a whole, by developing the skills to be a good and faithful husband, father and mentor to their family.

Isaac's House
P. O. Box 489
Corvallis, MT 59828
Phone: (406) 642-9849
Email: isaacshse@aol.com

for additional copies of **His Poetry,**
please go to Amazon.com

Will Harper can be emailed at info@rufreeindeed.com

rufreeindeed.com

(As of the time of this printing, the site was under construction. Please check back periodically.)

Printed in the United States
130093LV00001B/418-1500/P